SUPERNOVA

Anya Lia Munnelly

Copyright © 2012 Anya Munnelly.

Cover art by Mia Henderson©

All rights reserved.

ISBN: 9798471744684

Published by Amazon UK.

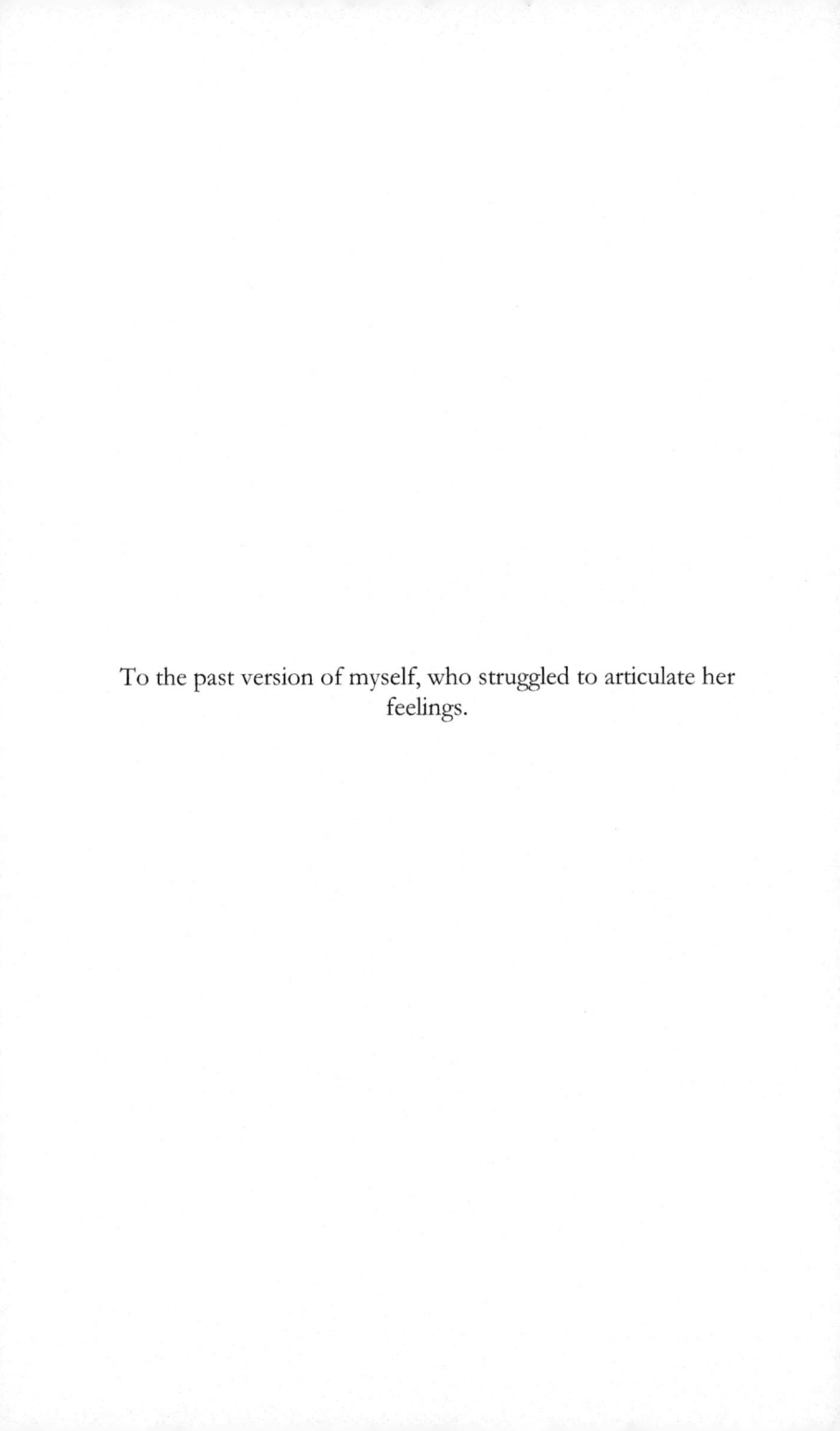

To the past version of myself, who struggled to articulate her feelings.

CONTENTS

catch a falling star.
   being in love.   *page 1*

across the sky.
   long distance and travel.   *page 28*

the end of our universe.
   breakups and heartbreak.   *page 45*

personal space.
   society, insecurity and grief.   *page 110*

into the void (tw)
   depression and mental health.   *page 127*

man on the moon.
   boys get sad too   *page 154.*

written in the stars.
   fate, destiny and prosperity.   *page 174..*

i want to write words,
ones that are sprung from my truth.
i want to fashion them into a design,
to inspire our damaged youth.

i want my words to resonate harshly,
and make the reader well up inside,
because they know the pain i felt,
writing down these neurotic cyanides.

my toxicities and my failings,
the life lessons i'm learning each day,
<u>i want</u> the world to see my pain,
and i want to help take theirs away.

my mission to space.

catch a falling star.

if this
is what love really feels like,
then maybe
i do believe in magic.

-witchcraft

SUPERNOVA

i loved him
the way a flower
was loved by a bee,
and the earth loved by the sun.
neither could survive
without the embrace
of the other,
and neither would be here,
if they didn't have
one another.

   -need you

you're the type of person,
i want to lay with
in the sand, on a beach, late at night.
looking only,
to the moonlit glare of the sky,
sparkling and exposing
the reflections of the water ripples.
i want to count each wave,
and dip our toes in the water.
seeing if the ocean,
can handle us.

> - *riding the wave*

SUPERNOVA

you taught me that love,
should be easy.
inexplicably,
undeniably,
<u>easy.</u>

we sat on the garden swing;
the night was utterly black.
my head laid on your legs,
as we motioned forwards and back.
my green dress wavered occasionally,
in the drift of the night time breeze,
i shivered unknowingly,
so, you placed your jumper on me.
i looked up from your thighs,
and smiled to your face,
you bent down towards my lips,
as yours found their rightful place.
i sat up for a moment,
and moved to straddle your lap,
as you pushed away my hair,
placing your arms around my back.
the next thing that you said to me,
made me realise you were the one,
"the sky may be dark tonight,
but my love; you are the sun".

-the perfect dream

SUPERNOVA

i don't know
where,
when,
why,
or what,
made me love you

but it did.

SUPERNOVA

a stubborn heart is a damaged one.

afraid to fall,
but not scared to fly.
conscious of the wind,
but in love with the sky.

SUPERNOVA

i looked at your hand on the steering wheel
and thought about its touch.
how it felt running through my hair,
making me fall in love.

and you laughed when our song came on,
then started singing the words.
the two of us began screaming the lyrics,
without a care in the world.

so, you turned, and you looked at me,
as we both began to smile,
because nothing ever changes,
even when i haven't seen you in a while.

yet a soft, sadness sat inside me,
not knowing how you truly feel,
but in that moment, i realised it was love,
just seeing your hand on the steering wheel.

-driving me crazy

if you cannot go a day,
without thinking about it,
except when toxic,
or causing you pain -

<u>it is,</u>
worth fighting for.

SUPERNOVA

as this love
bleeds
from our veins,
galaxies above us
burn
without refrain.

-star crossed

when your heart is too heavy,
let me carry you.

when your mind isn't safe,
let me protect you.

when you don't feel enough,
let me remind you.

> *-just let me love you.*

SUPERNOVA

he reignited the dead flames inside of me,
even if only for a short while,
until my wicks
burned out again.

SUPERNOVA

i love you
more than words
can allow.
is that
what they meant,
by words
aren't enough?

SUPERNOVA

i am in love with everything you are,
you were
and are yet to be.
but to learn this,
you must first
stay.

-catch me

SUPERNOVA

in a world,
where there's
so much to do.
i'd still rather sit,
and count stars
with you.

-wrong era

SUPERNOVA

one day someone will look at you with matchstick eyes.
setting alight every time they see your face. they'll love you
unconditionally, no matter where you've been or what
you're going through. embers of your love will sit in their
eyes when you're apart and reignite when you're together
again.

just wait,
everyone has their eternal flame.

if time is endless
then baby don't rush.
your heart will heal,
when it's ready again, to love.

    -when you least expect it

SUPERNOVA

thankyou
for loving me:
on my worst,
my best,
when weary,
when unsteady,
and most importantly,

<u>at all.</u>

the heat from a fire,
a blanket,
a hot cup of tea,
could never surround me
and make me warm,
the way you do.

    -heat of the moment

SUPERNOVA

yet no matter what,
you do.
i'm sure
i'll still love,
the worst
of you

        -my biggest flaw

SUPERNOVA

happiness isn't necessary
to keep the heart alive
the embers of a unity
will still burn fire in her eyes.

SUPERNOVA

it will always be him.
on a rainy day,
in late june or may.
in the distant future,
or 10am tomorrow.
with a lover on my arm
or yielding heartbreaks
evil charm,
it will still,
always,
be him.

i knew i hadn't made a mistake,
in how i was feeling,
when i looked into his eyes,
and staring back,
wasn't just him,
but myself.
his soul mirrored mine,
and then,
we both shattered,
simultaneously.

-broken lovers

SUPERNOVA

it had been years.
years of what ifs.
years of maybe one days.
years of people getting sick of us,
sick of us saying we were just friends,
when we were very clearly more than that.

we fooled nobody,
nobody but ourselves.

-it was love

we always missed each other.
finding ourselves with someone other.
whenever our hearts aligned,
it was always the wrong time.

but i'm hoping that one day
love will find a way
we can leave the hurt in the past,
saving the best for last.

SUPERNOVA

you made everything matter.

across the sky.

SUPERNOVA

i don't know if
the reflections from the water,
the glistening of the ripples,
or the love in your eyes
were my favourite thing that day,

but i knew i wanted it forever.

-ocean crossed lovers

SUPERNOVA

near you,
or lost to sea.
far away,
or beside me.
i will forever
and always be,

<u>yours.</u>

SUPERNOVA

i just turned my light off. the room fell dark. the clockwork of the end of the day, marked by the exclusion of the light from my view. the stars shine through though. seen clearly in the windowpanes of the old attic room in which i lay. i count them out. one, two. and i slowly begin to tear up. three. four. because although we're miles apart. five. six. my stars and yours, they're the same no matter where we are.

- underneath the same sky.

'this message goes out to you,
tomorrow,
when you're upset,
and watching videos,
and not happy,
because you miss me.

i love you'

-long distance lullaby.

SUPERNOVA

sometimes i wonder
what it would be like,
to fall asleep next to him,
in my arms
instead of in his thoughts.

sometimes i wonder,
how it would feel,
to kiss him goodnight
instead of repetitive,
phone calls and goodbyes.

sometimes i wonder,
if he looks up at the moon,
taking in her beauty
and then i remember,
he does,
and
i'll be seeing him very soon.

-5 0 6 4

i waited at the arrival gates,
and checked that his flight had arrived.
it said bags had been delivered,
at 9:39.
which meant he was on his way to me,
and he was amongst this bustling crowd,
with a backpack, a suitcase and a smile,
to turn my world upside down.

he came through the doors with his cap on,
and the jacket he always wore,
his smile beaming from ear to ear,
and his dimples accompanied it all.
we bought a drink then got on the bus,
back to where i was living,
and the whole way home i felt closer,
than i ever had since the beginning.

-when home came to visit

SUPERNOVA

i closed my eyes at night
and i woke and you were still there.
i felt like i was dreaming
but i knew i wasn't,
by the brush of your hand through my hair

as you rolled to face me,
your eyes wide with the exhaustion,
you smiled willingly
and placed a kiss upon my forehead,
making me fall without caution.

we fell back asleep
awaking hours later,
and you held me tightly
before distance took you back again.
yet another, <u>see you later.</u>

-mine for the weekend

the exit sign stayed awake
as the entire plane slept,
and i stared at it momentarily
as if it meant i had never even left.

thinking to myself, what if i jump
or what if i could fly
i could run straight back to him
and then i'd never have to say goodbye.

there was an occasional hum of the assist bell,
and the light of the seat belt sign,
couples lay close to one another,
as i was leaving him behind.

because this distance standing between us,
breaks my heart each time
and if i could holt the hurting,
i think we'd be just fine.

landing down in the airport,
just felt like i'd lost part of myself
and that everything just been became history,
the moment i took my case
                              from the conveyer belt.

SUPERNOVA

i howl at the moon,
hoping he hears me,
through the mustiness of the sky.

i become blinded by the sun,
hoping he'll see me,
through the worlds lighter eyes.

the yellow meadow fields
where his parents
taught him to ride a bike,
is the place i think about
before i fall asleep every night.
i envision us standing there,
as the sun sets,
with her auburn colours.
the gentle breeze
and the sway of the trees,
unifying us as lovers.

SUPERNOVA

dimly lit streets, on warm clammy nights,
the view of the landscape, kissed by the moonlight.
the hum of the bus, rattles, trembles as we move,
the memories in my life that i don't want to lose.

the stars up above, clouded by the dark,
the traffic lights, red, stand and take their mark.
the roads are empty now, night-time has begun,
but the glamour of the city lights, dance and have their fun.

the trees sway in the tender breeze, side by side,
the fear of losing all of this, aches and pricks my eyes.
the houses have gone to sleep, their insides seemingly hollow.
shop signs say, "closed right now, we'll see you again tomorrow".

my journey coming to an end, as the bus starts to slow
i sit here by myself, as i've watched everyone else go,
i look around and see the streets, feeling quite alone,
this place might not be incredible, but this place is my home.

-leeds

leaving home wasn't the hard part,
nor was leaving my friends,
or my mother.
it was not knowing,
when, or even if,
i'd find peace in somewhere other.

SUPERNOVA

leaving behind all i held dear,
choosing you as my life,
cutting ties with the old me,
sliced through with a sacrificial knife.

all i had remaining was history,
and the remnants of yesterday.
i had nothing left of my previous adventures,
but i got to hold you in my arms that way.

-i gave everything

there's a sacrificial emblem,
wavering above my head.
to show how courageous i had been,
to leap into your world instead.

-immigrant

sometimes home isn't a place,
it isn't these four walls,
and a roof.
sometimes home isn't family,
it's not your bloodline,
dna isn't bulletproof.

and sometimes home isn't a city,
nor a town,
or place to go.
sometimes when life gives you very little,
a home,
is quite simply,
<u>the people that you know.</u>

-homesick

true love isn't fazed by distance.

the end of our universe.

it's hard to let go of something in your mind, that your heart has already decided to hold forever.

he held me in his arms that night
and promised that he'd stay.
yet here we are gathered
to lay,
this love to rest.

-the day you left

i can never quite explain the sensation,
of feeling this type of arduous pain.
it hurts to the core and leaves me lifeless,
corruptions and explosions inside my brain.

as i lay on the bathroom floor,
enfolded into this self-woven ball,
no air in my lungs to catch a second,
no momentum to rise, so i can fall.

my nails they clutch the inside of my palms,
making dents on my cold shaken skin,
they're red raw with this unkind pain that i feel,
and the darkness very quickly bleeds in.

who cares if you don't see him again?
so what if it's over and done?
you'll find someone else who'll fill his place,
you can be someone else's second to none.

don't you see baby girl, it's just part of life,
you win some and the others you lose.
but i never thought i'd lose you at all,
i didn't prepare to not be your muse….

SUPERNOVA

….so i lay here breathless,
tears falling harder by the minute.
as i think about my day-to-day mannerisms,
and life without you in it.

it's just puppy love they keep telling me,
it'll all soon fade away,
but my house isn't a home, without a dog and bone,
and you here at the end of the day.

i don't expect anyone else to understand,
and i'm going to hoist the whole of the blame,
but as bronte said in her works of art,
<u>'whatever our souls are made of, his and mine were the same'.</u>

-soulmates

SUPERNOVA

i wonder
if the stars knew,
when our love
was finally over.

i wonder
if their lights
faded out,
and exploded in **supernova.**

SUPERNOVA

my veins,
they pulsate,
a daunting blue.
not with blood,
but with the loss,
of you.

SUPERNOVA

"he's not coming back, is he?"
 i wept into my best friends' arms.

"nobody can say." he replied

that word,
nobody.
nobody,
not even us.

my existence became confusing,
the moment we were no longer together.
yet if true love could have saved us,
we would have lived forever.

-when love isn't enough

i turned on the central heating,
and filled the bathtub.
stripped my clothes,
unclasped my hair,
and knelt in the water.
the warm twinge drew me under,
i soaked my face,
and accidentally filled my lungs.
i sat up coughing and laughing,
at what i'd just done.
then i stared at the tiles on the wall,
and with a single glance,
a lifetime of memories,
arose from the tank.

remember the time we took a shower?
we held one another,
under this waterfall tower?
i slumped over drunk,
and you picked me up.
tried to speak into your eyes,
but my words got stuck.
then you told me you loved me,
always and forever,
but where are you now?
we're not drowning together.

-heart beats to nothing. (h20)

SUPERNOVA

if i die before you wake,
i want you to know
i spent every hour of the day,
wishing you'd find your way home.

and by 'wake' i don't mean from slumber,
but from the love we left behind,
both wasting time pondering
and losing ourselves, one at a time.

-remember me

i remember shaking my head,
laughing,
and saying
"you're a fool,
if you think,
i could live without you."
i meant every word.
because i'm still alive,
but no longer living.

-life after our death

SUPERNOVA

what i'd give
for one more day
one more smile
more words to say.
what i'd give
for us two lovers
one more night
under the covers.
what i'd give
for one more dance
one more bottle
another chance.
what i'd give
for you back home
where you belong
so, we're not alone.
what i'd give
to see your face
to hear your voice
feel your embrace.
what i'd give
to sit with you
talk all night
a kiss or two.
what i'd give
to start again
to have you back
my boy again...

-anything

SUPERNOVA

it's hard to say
i loved you once,
when once
is now all
we have.

SUPERNOVA

i try to forget,
and lie to myself every day.
but you were the one,
and i let you get away.

SUPERNOVA

it's your small handwriting,
in old musky cards,
saying we'll always find our way back,
no matter how seemingly hard.

it's the memory of your body,
wearing these clothes that i hold.
it's the jewellery-station on my dresser,
seeing your name written in gold.

it's the dozens of photographs,
that i have hidden away,
but the ones i can't help crying over,
after a particularly difficult day.

it's the bumping into our old friends,
saying 'hey how are you?'
but the elephant in the room,
our breakup a complete taboo.

it's your scent on another man,
in the same cologne you would wear,
it's the looking at myself in a mirror,
and wishing your reflection was standing there.

it's the films we used to love,
or the ones we watched together,
remembering how you watched me weep,
when noah and ally found forever.

anyway, what i'm trying to say is,
it's not the loss of you on my mind.
it's the pieces of our love,
the fragments that you left behind.

SUPERNOVA

the weight
of your name alone,
bears wounds
and scars,
love-stricken
and broken hearts,
endless lost opportunities,
and a fragile,
once unstoppable,
unity.

-heavy

SUPERNOVA

our collisions of character,
embroidered emotions,
intertwined irregularities,
desperately loving devotions.

our serendipitous smiles,
along with arduous apologies,
creating idiosyncratic fate,
in science, just two similar anomalies.

loving you was life changing.
losing you was soul breaking.

-juxtaposition

SUPERNOVA

i woke up a little breathless,
a lump lodged in my throat.
a heavy weighted chest,
from that unconscious anecdote.

as the dream i'd just witnessed,
wasn't a dream at all,
more of a horror film in my mind,
that i wish i hadn't recalled.

and tears fell from my eyes,
the moment that they opened,
because watching you give me up,
made me wish i hadn't awoken.

and although it wasn't real life,
in reality, you still didn't stay,
but the reminder of how you hurt me,
was the worst way to start my day.

-nightmare

SUPERNOVA

i love you
but you broke me.
i care for you
but you left me.
i'll always remember us,
whilst you forget.
i'll long for one more smile,
or just a complete reset.

SUPERNOVA

if someone asked me
to define
the cause of my heartbreak,
a million thoughts
would cross my mind.
but the simplest way
to explain it,
would be admitting that
i desire something,
that will never again,
be mine.

i wish i had savoured the words
that fell from your lips,
as though they were
little droplets of liquid gold.
because how i hunger for them,
now that your body,
and your kiss,
are no longer here to hold.

SUPERNOVA

i didn't always treat him the way i should've,
and i know that now.

i didn't always show him enough patience,
i didn't always take his words seriously,
i didn't always listen close enough,
i didn't always say the nicest things,
and i know that now.

i didn't always act fairly in arguments,
i didn't always show him enough gratitude,
i didn't always kiss him to show my affection,
i didn't always say how i really felt about him,
and i know that now

i didn't always love him hard enough.

i just wish he knew, <u>that i know that now.</u>

just two stubborn,
broken hearted
people,
who found each other,
then lost it all.

-strangers again

SUPERNOVA

i was the indigo,
in your monotone sky.
but purple,
wasn't your favourite colour,
so that's where lovers
now come,
to die.

SUPERNOVA

i took out the draw from under my bed,
and found old things that time had forgot.
i held them in my arms for a little while,
because now these memories, are all i've got.

and the stupidest things just made me smile,
like the jumper you left in my house,
because back then i loved wearing a piece of you,
and now time has all but run out.

yet i'm trying to part with the little things,
like the necklace you bought for valentines,
but wearing it just makes me feel safer,
as though your arms are wrapped around mine.

and as i sat going through my many things,
i found the pyjama bottoms you always wore,
taking me back to breakfast in the mornings,
when the world was just simple and pure.

and each time i find something that links to you,
it takes me back to the very first day,
when you walked in the park and sat beside me,
the day you took my heart away.

-hoarder

SUPERNOVA

i couldn't listen
to that song anymore,
nor even read the lyrics aloud.
every line,
felt like it was screaming your name,
and the echo,
of what you left behind,
is too loud.

the only time i see you now,
is when i dream,
and that's bittersweet.
because although i see your for awhile
when i awake,
you're still out of my reach.

-dreamcatcher

SUPERNOVA

maybe it wasn't love,
maybe it was an addiction
and i'm just having withdrawal symptoms.
or maybe it was,
and there's no form of rehab
to help me.

we put up our walls,
to keep out the pain,
our hearts have had enough.

but those same walls,
drove us both insane,
as they also kept out
the love.

               -barricades

SUPERNOVA

part of me is angry at you,
for giving up on all we had built.
and doing it so easily,
walking away,
before our flower began to wilt.

but the most part of me is broken,
from the mistakes i made.
the remedies to our love i didn't take.
for not fixing up the bill,
and for letting you pay.

i know you'll be re-reading their messages.
looking back on old photographs.
and the videos they hit differently,
seeing their smile formulate or watching them laugh.
and you'll stay awake tossing and turning,
thinking about certain nights.
the ones spent drunk, or cosy in bed,
they'd pull you closer and squeeze you tight.
i know you still sleep in their jumper,
and listen to their favourite songs.
you want to still feel close to them,
not acknowledging they're actually gone.
i could try preaching and telling you,
to forget about their compassionate kiss.
but that would just be hypocritical,
because what do you think made me write - this?

-the process

SUPERNOVA

our love, a labyrinth.
an eternal maze.
our struggles, never ending
driving us insane.

another wrong turn,
or maybe that was right?
we won't know 'till we find the end,
but the end is never in sight.

SUPERNOVA

if love doesn't last forever
then where on earth does it go?
does in linger in only one of us
or do both parties finally let go?
if we let go does it float up,
and where does it drift away?
like a balloon in the wind
or bottle in the ocean
does someone else find our concealed dismay?

-where does broken love go?

SUPERNOVA

being in love with someone
when it isn't mutual,
and they don't care for you the same,
is parallel to
standing in a drought,
and waiting for the rain.

it's okay to be in love with someone,
who once was,
yet no longer is.
because people change,
they don't stay the same,
and you can't love,
what is <u>lost.</u>

from the second that you left,
and i watched you walk away,
i thought about our memories,
back to the very first day.

the minute i saw your back turn,
and walk towards the door,
my heart felt like a punch bag,
my knees took me to the floor.

i took one last look at you,
because i knew this was goodbye,
then you walked away without me,
and i couldn't even open my eyes.

the thought of you not here with me,
or that i'd never see your face
was enough to make my whole heart ache,
and enough to make me break.

the darkness tightened around my soul
and i found it hard to breathe,
if you loved me so much like you said you did,
why, did you just... leave?

-losing my best friend

SUPERNOVA

sticks and stones
may break your bones
but my love
would <u>never</u> have hurt you.

the person who will break you the most,
is not your epic love,
it's not that person who swept you off your feet,
who you spent years with,
and who crushed you when they left.
it's the person who made you believe,
that you were worth loving again.
who built you back up,
showed you how to feel happiness,
who promised they wouldn't do the same,

and did.

-the person after

we stood in a room,
with two locked doors,
you had my key,
and i had yours.

-no escape

SUPERNOVA

i was the strike of a match,
i lit us up in the darkness,
and burned bright,
on behalf of both of us.
but he was made,
of gasoline,
so, we both perished.

tonight, i lay thinking of you
whilst you lay with her.
i lay restless through the night,
and you fall asleep without a care.
i toss and turn,
staying on your side of the bed.
whilst you ruffle between the sheets,
making love to her instead.

SUPERNOVA

i found out all his favourite tv shows
and which was his side of the bed.
that he likes his coffee without milk,
but will have two sugars instead.

i found out about his family
and i learned all his favourite songs.
and at night he likes to lay on the sofa,
falling asleep with the fire and tv on.

i found out the way his lips feel.
that one day he wants 2 kids of his own.
the nickname they gave him in the navy,
and the reason he decided to come home.

i found out that he twitches in his sleep,
that i was saying his surname the wrong way.
and i learned that when he orders mcdonald's,
he gets the chicken burger with mayonnaise.

i found someone i paid attention to,
someone who made life feel secure
but when all was said and done,
                                      he still chose her.

SUPERNOVA

you have not yet asked for my forgiveness.
maybe you never will
but i grant it,
in hope you'll carry it,
with a heavy heart,
to prevent it happening,
to anyone else.

SUPERNOVA

never again,
look into another woman's eyes,
and hand her a falsehood,
of love.

she will carry it forever,
an empty casket,
mourning the death,
of the non-existent.

i had all the qualities
of someone
who could keep him safe,
and happy,
for an eternity.
the problem is,
he didn't believe in forever.

SUPERNOVA

i had disguised his failings
for a while now,
making excuses for his idiocy
by hiding them,
behind my own.

SUPERNOVA

he pushed me away
frequently,
in fear
my heart would break.

but opposed,
to his ill knowledge
was the fact,
that it wasn't his decision,
to make.

SUPERNOVA

i never stopped
loving you.
but you stopped,
giving me reason to.

SUPERNOVA

i could never hate those
that i have loved.
only feel sorrowful,
not for myself
but for them.
they took a pure heart,
a rare form of love,
and chose it not.

SUPERNOVA

my tears dried up,
the same day,
your honesty did.

my heart stopped beating as fast,
the same day,
yours lied to me.

my faith in you died,
the same day,
your innocence did.

her tired sunken eyes
hypnotised,
petrified
and terrified,
of his never-ending lies.
yet completely and utterly,
mesmerised
by the way a bird flies,
and the clouds,
in the misleadingly beautiful skies.
her body sits paralysed
harrowingly cries,
as she tries,
wonders why,
the cutting of ties
was even necessary at all.

-she loved the world until you left her

SUPERNOVA

i thought i had healed with time,
that i was accepting of what we are,
but i was reminded tonight of your smile,
and the knowledge it's for her.

i clutch the necklace you gave me,
and sob into your old baggy jumper,
laying where it all began,
when you came to visit that very first summer.

your silhouette lingers everywhere,
and the ghost of you is all i have left,
looking to the mirror, i see you smiling at me,
as you retreat from the shower to get dressed.

and our mattress on the floor is a bed now,
i've finally found my feet,
i've resurrected all the death inside me,
and i'm everything you needed me to be.

i can't help but reminisce it all,
as tears escape my reddening face,
four years of my life, loving by your side
and yearning for your warm embrace.

you'd love the life i could give you now,
but i know darling it's too late,
you're happy with someone else tonight,
and because of that,
i find my greatest mistake.

-finding forever at the wrong time

i feel like there's a void in me,
that my soul is still weakened,
i just want to wake up tomorrow,
and be someone else's reason.

-help me heal

SUPERNOVA

last time
i was holding on
this time
i'm moving on.

yet unlike the rest,
i broke his chain of regret.
as i could never hate,
only love.

-i refuse to be like the rest

SUPERNOVA

the curve of my hips,
the taste of my lips,
the quiet lives bliss,
true loves kiss,
any given wish,
and days like this,
all of them,
you'll miss.

it's not that i'm not ready to love,
because my heart
is always ready.
it's the fact
i'm not ready to lose,
another,
after already losing so many.

SUPERNOVA

people ask me,
about the complexity
of what love means.

they say,
they think they'll never
find it.

but finding it,
is nowhere near as hard,
as losing it.

SUPERNOVA

i waited too long
to tell you i loved you.
so, this is both
my confession,
and apology.

SUPERNOVA

characteristics of a person,
can be found in someone else.
those traits you fell in love with,
will belong to someone other.
he wasn't the only one.
there <u>will</u> be another.

-it's going to take time

maybe, you were just meant to be my muse.

i find him hard to talk about now,
at first,
he was the only thing
i would speak on.
his loss,
the pain i felt,
the memories i missed.
i vocalised my pain
and i told the world.
but as time grows older
and our love grows colder,
thinking about him,
seeing old photos,
videos,
hearing our laughs-
it hurts harder,
not as fearsomely
but harder.

he was everything.
and i lost him.

-accepting it

promise me you'll love her.
unconditionally, love every inch of her.
cherish every smile she makes,
and every breathe she takes.
promise me you'll make her laugh
when she's all but ready to cry.
promise me whenever she's hurt,
you'll heal her,
by holding her.
disregard yourself
and look after her heart over your own.
promise me that whenever times get tough,
you won't walk away and call it quits.
promise me no matter who tries to intervene,
and break you down.
promise me you won't let them.
because no girl,
should ever have to endure the pain,
the pain i felt,
when i lost you.

-make it worth it.

SUPERNOVA

in the end
you were
the making
of me.

-exploding in supernova.

personal space.

SUPERNOVA

and when he closed the door
and said the last goodbye,
she looked in the mirror
and asked herself *'why'?*

i used to believe in fairy tales,
then a godfairy granted my wish,
she showed me the truth behind the masks,
and gave me a true loves kiss.
yet it wasn't all i'd hope for,
the world didn't consist of prince charmings
just alcoholism, heartbreaks,
drugs and self-harming.
i wasn't running from the ball,
i wasn't running from true love,
i was running from the toxic society
that taught me i wasn't enough.

- *a world in cinders*

injustice in society,
even in this modern age.
innocent lives being taken,
by our own manmade plague.

racism and discrimination,
piercing lives like a dagger.
we need to abolish this *shit* completely.
black lives matter.

-supporting the BLM movement

no woman,
no person,
should feel the weight,
of danger,
purely sprung,
from the
presence of a man.

but that is the sad reality.

-unease. in memory of sarah everard.

SUPERNOVA

laying in the bathroom,
hair soaked through
hoping the bubbles,
will tell me what to do.
revealing the skin,
that once was yours
paining myself,
by seeking out my flaws

i cradled the idea of being perfect,
more than i ever held myself.
but you can't ever be flawless,
if you neglect your own self health.

-pretty shouldn't hurt

the purple lines around your thighs.
that show the stretching of your skin.
the dark circles around your eyes,
that show the tiredness you bare within.

the dimpling of your imperfect complexion,
thats real term is cellulite.
the scars that you carry on your legs,
from your lonely, darkest nights.

the freckles around your face,
that join up when the weather is hot.
the love handled hips you have,
that you wish you could just cut off.

the smile lines that formulate on your face,
around your mouth, when you smile.
the dimples at the bottom of your back
that you haven't dared to look at in a while.

the number on the weighing scales,
that you hate to look at, at all.
your imperfections and insecurities.
are what make you b-e-a-u-t-i-f-u-l.

if the shape of my body
becomes more of a priority,
than the weight of the heart
i carry inside;
that's when
you no longer
deserve to be by my side.

- *i am worthy*

if you've ever stood
on the weighing scales
and closed
your judgemental eyes.
hoping the number
would be different
from what it was
the last time.
just know
it's perfectly normal
and that many of us
feel this way.
but just know someone
is going to love you,
no matter what
you weigh.

i'm tired.
i'm tired, yet not exhausted.
not of body,
but of mind.
whilst my body lays
and rests for the night.
my mind runs marathons
never stopping
never resting.

-mind runner

she gets attached too easy.
to everyone.
to anyone who shows,
that loving her is possible.
then she grieves when people leave.
but the truth is,
she hurts herself.
by always opening up.

-padlock heart

let your guilt
be the sacrifice
to the path
of a better life.

-forgiving myself

SUPERNOVA

the news spread like wildfire,
a diamond in the rough,
stood out in the world.
like ammo fired,
in a quiet area,
robust.
the siren sounds calling,
the breaking of our hearts,
one moment
of unclarity
leading to forever
apart.

-the accident. 07.03.2015

SUPERNOVA

six feet under
or perched above the clouds,
wherever your soul rests
i hope in me, it's proud.

SUPERNOVA

we're all just insignificant people
reaching,
for the same stars.

i used to torment myself with the idea of 'what if'. but i've
learned that to think this, is as hurtful as drinking cyanide.
it will starve you of breath, until there's nothing left to bring
you life.

into the void.

i am broken. not even entirely of body or mind. my soul is cracked, damned from the fates to which i have unknowingly propelled myself into. or rather, what was meant for me. my light only radiates when i allow it to. my darkness spends most of the time on the surface, snuffing out my vibrant visionaries. i love my life, which is contradictory really. it makes no sense, not to me, so most definitely not to anyone else. and so i write. i put words on a page, like a ruler to a graph, trying to figure out the square root of my own sanity. i have tried endlessly, to write what i feel inside, to articulate a formula to all of this. but my sums have been miscalculated many times, and i never seem to find the correct answer. the reason: life's grandeur, is not meant to have a destination, an answer, or a purpose. we live, and we die. we learn things along the way, and we frame our own lives into what we desire the most. my personal goals will forever and always be the serenity of my own soul, and the connection to someone else's, commonly labelled as love. the power behind two souls alike in compassion, is the most secure yet intimidating feeling. but security among the madness, defeats it all.

-square root of sanity

SUPERNOVA

do you dance with the devil?
can you see in the dark?
is your world unpredictable?
is your life falling apart?

can you see a tomorrow?
or just today?
is your heart still beating?
or taking your breath away?

time didn't hold my hand,
it liked to watch me fall.
because time would see me
breaking apart,
knowing
it could fix it all.

SUPERNOVA

day breaks
eyes closed
her bed covers
not exposed
daytime
hideaway
but the night-time
her getaway.
day dawns
still awake
sun comes up
another mistake.
day light
not again
bring back
her midnight friend
day by day
she fades to dust
the loneliest hours
    never enough.

-insomnia

SUPERNOVA

the bruises
became wider
and the aching
broke her apart
except the bruises
were invisible
and the aching
came from her heart.

SUPERNOVA

if you're seeing me breakdown,
if you're witnessing my tears,
just know that you must be incredible,
take my glass eyes as souvenirs.

she spent months
trying to evacuate herself.
escaping the brutality,
of the imminent explosion.
the catastrophe
and the heart ache,
that was her own
darkened emotions.

-at war with yourself

SUPERNOVA

tired of living,
but still alive.
bedroom curtains closed,
but you managed to open your eyes.

you know your body's hungry,
but you can barely even eat.
as you lay in the same position,
scared to get up of your feet.

and your bedroom ceiling is bored,
of seeing you hurt this way,
so maybe just close your eyes again,
<u>tomorrow's another day.</u>

-depressive episode

my hair was a mess today.
i sat in front of the mirror and cried.
not because of how i looked, i suppose,
but because of how broken i felt inside.

i didn't have the strength to sort it out,
so just tied it up instead,
and instead of carrying on with the day,
i just got back into bed.

i laid there and thought of it all,
and how you just left my life.
then i thought about the person before you,
and how i can never seem to get it right.

so i closed my eyes to take away the pain,
and threw my phone to the floor,
i don't think i can take another day like this
is all this living worth dying for?

-another bad day

SUPERNOVA

if i left this earth,
would you wish upon the stars for me?

she banged on the doors of heaven,
she begged to be let inside,
she lost her breath trying to scream,
yet felt no one could hear her cry.

she gathered the power to stop,
but kept wishing to be taken away,
so, she turned to a friend and told him…
…and he saved her life that day.

-pearly gates

SUPERNOVA

i took my favourite lyrics,
of a song that spoke to my soul.
and i inked them onto my skin,
because it made me feel whole.
as though the meaning of the song,
had sunk deep within,
and allowed me to finally breathe,
subtly expressing,
the pain i was in.

it's weird how one day
can change everything.
even just a moment.
one minute,
you're walking straight ahead.
the next,
you're at a standstill
and there's a car coming
and you're frozen,
can't move,
scared,
hearts beating,
minds whirling
and crash.
everything's in pieces.

-we all have car crash moments

SUPERNOVA

she packed her life into boxes,
as she lived from a suitcase.
her mattress on the floor,
more comfortable than the day before,
but not enough to take her pain away.
and her restless nights consumed her,
as her bedroom door stay closed.
tears dripping to the floor,
to hide her ongoing internal war,
and to release her anger on this place.

and within the day she smiled,
to create an impeccable act,
but she cried at moonlight,
as she tried to win her fight,
against everything she'd ever known.
and a home was something unfamiliar,
as she'd been pitched from pillar to post,
she lived her life in wonder,
would it be sunshine? would it be thunder?
and will the skies be blue or grey?

she sits and dreams of an ending,
a happily ever after, as they say,
maybe one day her heart will rest,
she'll kill the monster clinging to her chest,
and be rid of all the shame.
but within the dark she's guided,
by her friends, her family, her job,
one day she will win her race,
stop living from a *fucking* case
and unpack her life from boxes.

$-va^3$

SUPERNOVA

incurable heartache
food left on the plate
starving not eating
hardly left breathing
tears soak the bed sheets
eyes burn, can't sleep.
toss and turn each night,
this is just surviving,
go
and live your life.

SUPERNOVA

<u>nothing</u> is worth losing your life for.

at the end
of it all,
i lost myself
and that
was far worse,
than losing you

bad decisions,
lonely nights.
constant heartbreaks
countless fights.
effortless solitude,
and damaged goods.
your heart must suffer,
before it can love.

> *-pain **is** temporary*

there are days that i look at my skin
and the scars that it bears.
i look at them with pride,
because i'm alive,
despite these crazy affairs.
and there are days i look at my arms,
or my thighs
or my leg
and i don't see anything to be proud of,
i just see a broken girl instead.

-it's okay not to be

SUPERNOVA

it's late
and you're reading this
looking for something
to relate to how you're hurt.
instead of seeking reassurance
in these safe haven words,
how about you forget it all,
and put
yourself
first.

start by getting up before 3pm.
then try to make your bed,
don't worry if it's too much,
just try again tomorrow.
try every day,
until you manage it.
then freshen up,
put on a real set of clothes,
and face the world,
so you can get back
to being,
you.

    -one day at a time

she sold her dream
on paper sheets
ink-stained hands
and tried feet.
waiting tables
getting by
then going home
with tired eyes.
writing words
about how she felt
letting the world
share them as well.
then her alarm would ring,
the birds would sing,
another day would begin
and she'd do the same,
damn
thing.

-trying to make it

the epicentre
of her mind
was a chasm
of how she felt inside.
constantly
searching
learning
and realising-
damn,
i'm still alive.
and if there's reason
to all of this
then what
do i do now?
will my mind
one day be healed
and will the world
become mine,
somehow?

SUPERNOVA

i am strong
because i am in pieces.
i rattle,
i crumble,
i flake apart,
yet
i am still here

    -survivor

nobody is ever truly broken.
a lot of us feel the same,
if ever in doubt,
please reach out,
starting a conversation
helps take away the pain.

i promise

    -tell someone

SUPERNOVA

please be the first to stay.

-dear readers

man on the
moon.

SUPERNOVA

vapours and liquors
faded his soul
the saturation of his emptiness,
lo and behold,
stopped when his head fluttered,
when the smoke turned to mist,
nothing but those toxicities,
could make him forget,
her kiss.

-substance state of mind

he held potential,
    but also carried poison in his pocket.

SUPERNOVA

her heart and yours,
an explosion.
constantly unleashing fire.
when will you realise
that
true love
doesn't come from liars?

i know he feels compassion,
i know he needs an embrace,
i know he blames himself,
i know his smile is fake.
i know he yearns for harmony,
i know he thinks he is impure,
i know he savours the memories,
i know he will always love her.
i know he has a stubborn heart,
i know he probably cannot sleep,
i know he wants to end the fight,
i know his faith is weak.
i know he's lost his integrity,
i know his mind is a mess,
i know he hurts people for fun,
i know his heartache is suppressed.
i know he needs time in his life,
i know he needs to grow,
i know you're trying my love,
trust me darling, i know.

-i understand you

excusing your vulnerability,
by believing that it is invalid,
only increases the war zone,
between communication and peace.

SUPERNOVA

his heart bled open,
as though carved out by a knife,
his heart, his soul and his body,
were hers, he didn't think twice.

the weight of the world he carried,
inside the rock solid, metal case,
to shield him from the heartbreak,
his suppress his accidental mistakes.

and he didn't mean to hurt her,
he was only being himself,
he didn't realise his lack of admiration,
was going to surface amongst his stealth.

his eyes looked nowhere other,
he was well and truly hers,
but she couldn't be with him any longer,
they were young, only amateurs.

he didn't speak to anyone,
he kept it all hidden away,
because *god forbid*, he'd look weak,
but that's what he needed for her to stay.

he kept his hardcore persona,
to align with his way of life.
but slowly and surely, he lost her,
his girlfriend, his could have been wife.

i hope one day she comes back to him,
or he falls in love with someone else,
because his heart loves like no other,
.... but first he must love himself.

SUPERNOVA

they loved each other indefinitely,
there was no doubt about that.
but no matter how hard they tried,
the love just wouldn't come back.

because words had already been spoken,
other people's bodies had been undressed.
yet they held onto the pain they felt,
because it's all that they had left.

-separated soulmates. for jake.

it's not always supposed to be easy. <u>cry.</u>

SUPERNOVA

losing your love
created a sorrowful void.
but watching you lose yourself,
began an agony
i still cannot avoid.

-please take care.

SUPERNOVA

he had a troubled heart,
with a chaotic mind.
he was still dressing old wounds,
that resurfaced from time to time.

he had a brave exterior,
to hide his internal pain,
he was storing away his hurt,
gripping tightly to most the blame.

he seemed brazen on the surface,
and could part oceans with his smile,
but despite his convincing performances,
he was still emotionally fragile.

he fooled most that knew him,
except the ones that held him tight.
he desired harmony in his life,
and to end this constant fight.

someday he'll open his eyes,
and accept in the worlds wonder,
he'll navigate towards the sun,
and ignore the rain and thunder.

that day he'll feel weightless,
and his triumph will be notorious.
darling, one day you won't feel this way,
<u>one day you'll be victorious.</u>

SUPERNOVA

men hurt too.

you would reach out your hand,
and he wouldn't take it.
he'd fall off the grid,
and make you replace him.

he smoked until he was faded,
taken by the mist.
he'd drink until he was ruthless,
and many felt the brutality of his fist.

he was lost in a cave of wonders,
crazed by the mountains and the shores.
a whole new world,
going places he'd never been before.

he loved the freedom of running,
or cycling somewhere quiet.
he'd sit, he'd smoke, and he'd listen to his songs,
whilst his internal battles would run riot.

life was all but kind to him,
but he'd never tell you that himself.
he'd wait until death was calling,
to admit that he needed your help.

yet his smile was so infatuating,
and when sober, he held the potential-
to free himself of the toxicity,
but he deemed himself inconsequential.

so, now i'm talking to you directly,
because all that you need to know,
is even though you think this world doesn't need you,
mine does. so please don't let go.

SUPERNOVA

his body aches around mine,
as he's bearing the pain,
from someone else.
for although his love
surrounds me,
it's not together as one,
so i essentially
lay here,
by myself.

      -not really there

how do you think it made me feel,
knowing you gave up?
without goodbyes
you just closed your eyes
and decided enough is enough.
well, i'm glad we found your body,
lifeless on the floor.
because much later,
you'd of had your wish
and death would have been yours.

-tough love

SUPERNOVA

the sun kissed reflections in my eyes
of happier, warmer times in our lives.
i still see dawning after darkness,
as this feeling inside me, never dies.

oh, i wonder, oh i wonder
do i ever cross your mind?
as the rain is falling softly from my window,
will your smile ever again, be mine?

-two sides of the story

written in collaboration with Adam Maguire.

i loved him even more
on his worst days.
not in a narcissistic, cruel way
that meant i enjoyed
his pain, siding with mine.
but because
he was ruthlessly fragile,
and needlessly vulnerable.
and that meant,
he was indefinitely comfortable,
beside me.

SUPERNOVA

to fight his demons
he used people
as distractions.
one by one
he left them broken
the way
she
had left him.

he desired for me to hate him
to make it easier
to allow himself
to feel justified,
in all he had done.

-i still don't

SUPERNOVA

falling
is part of flying,
losing
is part of loving.
crying
is part of healing,
breaking
is part of bruising.

written in the
stars.

SUPERNOVA

and then one day,
i looked out on the horizon,
yet no longer saw your face.

live your life,
and do what you must do.
then when the sun rises,
i promise i'll think of you.

and if life is meant to be,
the way that we hoped for,
you'll come back to me
and we can rewind
to before.

-if it's meant for us

SUPERNOVA

just because i'll always love you,
doesn't mean i won't love another,
and the way i know this now
is that when i hear those love songs,
it's not your face i imagine,
laid between my covers.

you started a fire,
you burnt me,
scorched my life,
and flickered in the embers,
that you left behind.

but you failed to remember,
a phoenix,
rises
from ash.

    -reborn

SUPERNOVA

phoenix feathers
flutter in my subconscious,
tickling and reminding,

that i will rise again.

SUPERNOVA

if all else fails,
my heart was strengthened,
from your loss.
and next time,
it will beat harder,
for someone else.

one thing i've learnt,
in all my searching,
for a new happiness,
the reason for all of this,
is that there are some things,
some things in life,
that won't ever become less painful,
no matter how hard you try.

but
that's
okay.

SUPERNOVA

what would be the point,
in giving up,
on something we weren't ready for?
as that is what defines,
and holds the beauty
of spontaneity.

SUPERNOVA

no one
in your life is a mistake.
there's too many of us in this world,
for destiny
to be fake.

-7 billion

SUPERNOVA

you may no longer
be mine
but part of me
will forever
and always
be yours.

SUPERNOVA

if two souls
alike in compassion
lose one another.
i'd like to believe
that destiny will intervene
and one day
bring them back to each other.

-love finds a way

what we want,
and what's meant for us,
are very rarely the same.
we don't get to decide.
although most of us have tried,
to cheat our way, out of this game.

-denying fate

you are not the person you were two years ago, nor will you ever be again. you evolve and you change with every passing day, every experience and every beat of your heart. forever learning and forever cleansing.

so, stop drowning yourself in emotions that the old you created.

sometimes in life,
when the cards you're dealt,
are not desirable,
and don't create the greatest hand.
the only thing,
we can do to prosper,
is reshuffle the deck,
and <u>try again.</u>

SUPERNOVA

courage
is just making fear
a responsibility.

life isn't a rehearsal,
we don't get to do this again.
there's no reset button.
no rewind features.
this is it.

do what you love.
do what makes you happy.

if pieces of a jigsaw were missing,
it could never be whole.
so don't waste time on parts of you
that don't have a completion goal.

    -dream wisely

SUPERNOVA

you're never
going to be ready
for what's meant for you.
if we could anticipate
our forever,
we wouldn't want it as much.
infinity,
is supposed to creep up on you.

SUPERNOVA

you'll never get past the first step,
if you have a false start.
don't move faster than you are able,
think about your abilities, before you depart.

SUPERNOVA

you could manifest
the entire world,
with infinite things
to achieve.
you could conjure
your own happiness,
if you just
let
yourself
believe.

SUPERNOVA

this universe
hands us the same fate
time after time.
learning from your mistakes
is *the only way*
to move on.

have you ever sat outside
and looked at the night sky?
something about the way it feels
makes you come to life.

-aurora

i know we don't get a happy ever after
and i know we're a beautiful disaster,
but i do know
we'll be alright.

the moonlight delved into its depths once more,
as the sun painted her scarlet colours.
they danced in unison, as i watched,
them in harmony with one another.

and for a moment as i was standing there,
everything finally made sense,
if the sun and moon can be friends today,
then maybe i'll find you again.

-the moment i knew i would be okay.

SUPERNOVA

she often fell asleep with the light on,
her laptop beside her in bed,
words scribbled on the screen that she'd written,
and emily bronte quotes circling her head.

she highlighted her favourite lines from books,
and looked back when her days were bleak,
she found comfort in words of the previous,
and bought a new classic novel each week.

she tried to find grace in the pages,
then she tried to write down her own,
she wanted to be like one of the admired,
and that's when typography, became her home.

she released it all from her troubled mind,
her thoughts imprinted like an ink stain,
quickly the pages became her livelihood,
and her writing helped stop the pain.

THANKYOU.

SUPERNOVA

Acknowledgements

For this book to be in your hands, it took the determination and support of many other people. I want to thank every single one of them. This may take a while...

Firstly, to the publishing company, that has brought my vision to life and helped me create my dream debut poetry collection. To Amazon for pushing the book out into the world and allowing me to use your platform to promote and release my words. I've had complete creative freedom the whole way, and I'm very grateful for the opportunity.

To all the amazing agents, creators, poets and writers who have aided me in this journey, given me words of wisdom and pointed me in the correct direction to achieving the best book possible. From helping in the editing process to straight up tough love. Your own work inspires me every day- we're in this one together.

To my amazing friend and cover artist, Mia Henderson, for creating the beautiful art for this book and listening to my ramblings of vague descriptions yet bringing my visions to life so effortlessly. Your talent has always amazed me, and I wouldn't have trusted anybody else. Thank you. (hendodoodles on Instagram)

To my mum Kathryn, dad Ronan, and all other family members - whom to which, this book is probably a complete surprise. A lot of what I do, I do privately, and I've never fully explored my love for poetry and writing with you guys, but I hope this made you proud (and wasn't too hard to read). Without the upbringing and experiences, you gave me, I would never have found myself or been the woman I am today. I love each of you immensely.

All the group in Ireland (you all know who you are- there's too many of you to name individually) for accepting me in, creating some of the best memories and showing me so much light in darker times. You gave me a whole new meaning of 'home'.

My work colleagues at The Rose & Crown and The Purty Central. Especially Sue Encell, for being a second mother to me in times I needed it the most, I will always 'Look to You.' Along with Bryan Keogh, for being not only the best manager, but my best buddy over in Ireland.

To my **closest** friends, that I share my favourite life moments with, and who have done nothing but encourage and believe in my abilities for years now. You guys are the reason I love my life so much; Connor Baldwin, Phoebe Backhouse, Ben Moody, Macy Edward, Fiona Maynard, Will Dunnington, Harvey Mcgreavy-Gill, Matthew Adams, Adam Nicholson, Leanne Morrissey (Jayden, Jacqui and bump), Oliver Jones, Neil Kavagnah, Josh Backhouse, Luke Ambler, Harry Hughes, Skye Shaw (Theo and Kasen), Megan Mcgrath, Ethan Scott, Laura Mundy, Freyja Kuryliw, George Lythe, Scott Munnelly, Jenny Atack and Hannah Carter. Along with all my other close friends who I've not mentioned; your names are **all** running through my head, I haven't forgotten you- you know who you are!

To Ciara Reid, Chelsea Storr, Amber Robinson and Olivia McCann for always being a listening ear, a phone call away, and for seeing me through the toughest parts of this journey. You have never once given up on me and are the girlfriends I always dreamed of having.

To Gavin Connolly and Jack Saddington, for being the brothers I never had. Looking after me always and winding me up just as equally! I'm lucky to have you both.

To Henry Larkin, for being not only a muse in all of this, but a person whose soul soothes my own. I hope you loved this book; your encouragement is part of the reason I felt ready to share it with the world. I'd walk right down the line for you.

To Ellie Barrett, for being my leading lady, my best friend and constant carer! You look after me without hesitation, laugh when I want to laugh, and sit on doorsteps in the freezing cold when I need to cry. You are an angel to this world, and I hope me FINALLY achieving something, will make you super proud. I love you more than you know, and I wouldn't be here without you. (even if you did try killing me and breaking my foot).

To Jake Keogh (you thought i'd forgotten you didn't you), for being my missing piece, my better half and the most amazing friend I could ever ask for. You were there on THE worst days, you created some of the best and you will always be my living hero. Without your friendship and laughter, crying, drama and reassurance I wouldn't be who I am today. We did this one together (aided by a few thousand gallons of alcohol)! You truly deserve the world and more. I love you my twin flame.

To my muses, the people who helped spark emotion within me and lead me to the words in the first place. There are many of you. Some of you are friends with stories of your own, that you have allowed me to share. Some of you are strangers, who trusted me with your worries on my Instagram, and the most part of you, are the men I have adored the most. CB, MA and HH; thank you for allowing me to be in your life, showing me what it means to care and for loving me when you did. We all make mistakes, I myself - wish I could change many things about our stories, but I hope the pages of this book explain what I wish I could to you. (I doubt any of you are reading this though oops)

To each of you that reads, reposts, shares and engages with my work on my Instagram, Wattpad and TikTok. The strength your support and words give me is unparalleled. If you've purchased this and read this far, I really do owe it all to you.

And finally, but most importantly, to Adam Maguire-Walsh for being the biggest believer of me and my abilities from day one. You pushed me to begin this journey, you forced me to embrace the passion I have, and without your support, guidance, constant pushes and collaboration- none of this would have been possible. I hope I've made you proud. Thank you for choosing me to save. This books for you.

A x

Printed in Great Britain
by Amazon